God's Plan for You in the Bible

Book 1 – Old Testament
An ESL Bible Study

Nimmi Swamidass

God's Plan for You in the Bible

Bible stories – Genesis to Jesus, with ESL learning exercises

Book 1 – Old Testament

"For I know the plans I have for you," declares the LORD, "plans to prosper you and not to harm you, plans to give you hope and a future."

Jeremiah 29:11 (NIV)

Unless otherwise indicated, Scripture quotations are from New International Reader's Version (NIrV) Copyright © 1996 by International Bible Society.

ISBN-13:978-1478148883
ISBN-10:1478148888

Printed in the United States of America
Charlotte, SC, U.S.A.

Preface

God loves all people everywhere. *"For God so loved the world, that he gave his only Son, that whoever believes in him should not perish but have eternal life." (John 3:16, ESV)* He has wonderful plans for each person. Those plans can be fully realized only when we get connected to Him. Sin separates us from God. To be connected to Him, we need to first accept His wonderful plan of salvation through His Son, the Lord Jesus Christ.

One day, people asked Jesus, *"What does God want from us? What works does he want us to do?" Jesus answered, "God's work is to believe in the One he has sent." (John 6:28-29)* The purpose of this book, as well as Book 2 of New Testament stories, is to present the One we need to believe. That One is the Lord Jesus Christ. Faith in Him is God's first desire for each one of us.

In *Romans 8:32,* we read, *"God did not spare his own Son. He gave him up for us all. Then won't he also freely give us everything else?"* My prayer is that you will come to faith in Jesus Christ and accept His plan to make you part of His family. As you follow Him and His Word, the Bible, you will know the wonderful plans He has for you. You will be greatly blessed by God.

Nimmi Swamidass

CONTENTS

Introduction

In these lessons, we will be studying the **Bible** to know more about God. He loves you very much. He has wonderful plans for your life. We can learn many things from the Bible. Some of the things we will learn are:

- how the world was created,
- who is God,
- God's love for all people,
- how evil (sin) came into this world,
- God's plan to save us from punishment,
- who is Jesus,
- His life and teachings, and
- our forever future.

This book will also help you learn English. The vocabulary list will help you learn new words. There are questions at the end of each lesson. You will find the answers when you read the lesson. The answers are also at the back of the book. We will use the Bible as our 'text' book. Read each story from the Bible. Read the Bible in your own language also.

First, we will study about the Bible. God has told us in the Bible all we need to know about Him and His plan for our life. God loves all people everywhere. He wants us to know Him and love Him. He wants to forgive our sins. He wants a close relationship with us. He wants to bless us. He wants to give us joy and peace. He wants to help us. He wants us to live with Him forever.

God is all powerful. He can do anything. God knows all things. God is everywhere at the same time. God is Spirit. God is holy. God loves you. God has promised many blessings for all those who love and follow Him. We will learn about God and His wonderful plan for us. It is for all people, all over the world.

1.   God Speaks to Us

Bible Verse: *"God has breathed life into all of Scripture."*
(2 Timothy 3:16.)

The Bible is called the 'Holy Bible' because it is a **sacred** book. It is sacred because it is God's message to us. All the words in it are true. They are God's words. God is Truth. He cannot lie. So the whole Bible is true. The Bible says, *"All your words (God's) are true…" (Psalms 119:160.)*

God did not write it with His own hands. He gave His words to 40 different men to write the Bible. All the words in the Bible are God's Words. So, the Bible is also called the 'Word of God'. God **communicates** with us when we read the Bible.

The Bible tells us many things about God. It tells us that God created the universe and everything in it. We read how much God loves us. He desires to have a relationship with us. He wants to be our Father and take care of us.

The Bible has many 'books' in it. There are 66 books in the Bible. It is divided into the Old and New **Testament.** The Old Testament was written many years before Jesus Christ was born. In it we read about how the world was created. It tells us the history of the Jewish people. It tells us of God's plan for all nations.

The first four books in the New Testament give us the **biography** of Jesus Christ, God's Son. We can read about His life and what He taught. In the Bible we read that He came into this world to save us from our sins. We read that He is the way to heaven. The **rest** of the New Testament is about the early Christian church. It also tells us how to have a strong relationship with God.

In the Bible, we read about who God is, who man is and what is good and evil. From the Bible we can know how to have peace and joy in our life. We can know how to go to heaven. The Bible can help us have success in this life.

Vocabulary:

1. **Scripture**: sacred written words. The Holy Bible is the scriptures for Christians. It is God's word for all people
2. **sacred**: holy, belonging to God
3. **communicate:** to give the message; to connect
4. **Testament:** a covenant (firm agreement) between God and man
5. **biography:** written information about someone from their birth to death
6. **rest:** remaining; what is left

Fill in the blanks:

1. The Bible is a _____ book.
2. It is sometimes called the _____ of God.
3. All the words in the Bible are God's _____.
4. There are _____ books in the Bible.
5. The Bible has the _____ Testament and the _____ Testament.

Answer the following questions:

1. What is the 'Word of God?' _____
2. Why is the Bible called the 'Holy Bible'? _____
3. Why is the Bible called the 'Word of God'? _____
4. How can we know that God loves us? _____
5. Why did Jesus, God's Son, come to this world? _____

Core Sentences:

The Bible is God's Word.
The Bible is God's book.
God cannot lie.
The Bible, God's Word, is true.

2. God and Creation of Angels

Bible Verse: *"Praise him, all his angels. Praise him, all his angels in heaven. Let all of them praise the name of the Lord, because he gave a command and they were created." (Psalm148:2, 5)*

God:

God is **almighty.** He is all powerful. He is more powerful than anyone. God is everywhere. He knows everything. He is **Creator.** He created everything in **heaven**, on earth and under the earth.

God is personal. He has personality. He thinks, wills, feels and acts. The Bible tells us that God is **Spirit.** So, He is invisible. He is **immortal.** He lives forever. He does not have a physical body. He created man and woman like Him, but people have physical bodies.

God is **holy.** God hates **sin.** God says that sin must be punished. God is love. He loves people everywhere. He loves people of all nations. He wants all people to love Him and have close relationship with Him.

Angels:

We don't know exactly when God created angels. He probably created them before he created the world. Angels are servants of God. They are His messengers. They were created to **worship** and obey Him.

There was a very beautiful angel called Lucifer. Lucifer became very **proud.** The Bible says Lucifer wanted to be like 'the Most High'. He wanted to be God. There is only one God. No one else can be God. Lucifer rebelled against God. He sinned against God. Lucifer and the angels that followed him made war with God. Of course, God won. God is all powerful. Lucifer and his followers were expelled from heaven.

Lucifer became Satan. One meaning of Satan is 'enemy.' Satan is the greatest enemy of God. Satan and the angels who followed him are the evil spirits or demons. Satan wants people to disobey

God. God has prepared **hell** for Satan. All who don't follow God and His ways will be sent to hell. God does not want anyone to go to hell. God wants us to **repent** of our sins and believe in His Son, Jesus. We must decide to follow Him by obeying His Word, the Bible. Then He will accept us and welcome us into heaven.

Vocabulary:

1. **almighty:** all powerful, more powerful than anyone
2. **create:** make something from nothing
3. **heaven:** space above the earth; place where Jesus is now
4. **spirit:** not natural, like man; spiritual; not human
5. **immortal:** does not die
6. **holy:** without any sin; completely without any wrongdoing
7. **sin:** all wrong doing; not obeying God's words
8. **worship:** to honor God; to praise and serve God
9. **hell:** eternal punishment for Satan and his followers
10. **repent:** be sorry for wrong done and turn away from it

Fill in the blanks:

1. God is S _____. He does not have a physical body.
2. God is h _____. There is no evil in Him.
3. God is a _____. He is more powerful than anyone.
4. God is c _____. He made everything.
5. God is all-k _____. He knows everything.

Answer the following questions:

1. Who has more power than any spirit or person? _____
2. God is holy; what does He hate? _____
3. What did Satan do? _____
4. What was Satan's punishment? _____
5. What does Satan want us to do? _____

Core Sentences:

God is love. God is holy.
God hates sin. Sin must be punished.
Jesus Christ paid for our sins.

3.   God is the Creator

Bible Verse: *"'Lord and King, you have reached out your great and powerful arm. You have made the heavens and the earth. Nothing is too hard for you." (Jeremiah 32:17.)*

People believe different ways about the beginning of the earth. Let's see what the Bible says. The Bible is **absolutely** true.

We read in the Bible that God created the world and everything in it. He created everything in six days. He spoke and it was made. God is all powerful. He can do anything. We can read about **creation** in the Bible, in the book of Genesis. Genesis means "beginning."

On day 1, God made day and night. *Genesis 1:3-5.*
On day 2, God made the sky. *Genesis 1:6-8.*
On day 3, God made the land, sea, and all the plants.
    Genesis 1:9-13.
On day 4, God made the sun, moon and stars. *Genesis 1:14-19.*
On day 5, God made the sea creatures and birds.
    Genesis 1:20-23.
On day 6, God made the land animals. *Genesis 1:24-25.*

On the sixth day, God also created His most important and special creation. He created man and woman. In *Genesis 2:7,* the Bible tells us that God made man: *"Then the Lord God formed a man. He made him out of the dust of the ground. He breathed the breath of life into him. And the man became a living person."*

God created man to resemble Him. God created man holy, just like Himself. God created man to have **relationship** with Him. God is Spirit. God does not have a **physical body.** We read in the Bible that *"No one has ever seen God." (John 1:18.)*

On the seventh day, *"God finished the work He had been doing ..." (Genesis 2:2.)* He saw that everything He had created was very good. *(Genesis 1:31)*

God is a good God. God is a God of love. He loves people. He loves people all over the world. He made people to have close relationship with Him. He gave Adam and Eve the whole earth to **rule** over. They were very happy. But soon something very bad happened. They disobeyed God.

Vocabulary:

1. **reached out**: to stretch
2. **absolutely:** completely, 100%
3. **creation** (noun): something that has been created
4. **relationship:** to have a connection with; to be close to someone
5. **physical body:** body of flesh and blood, like that of humans
6. **rule:** to be in control of; in charge of; take care of

Fill in the blanks:

1. God created the world and _____ in it.
2. God created the _____ and the _____
3. God created man and _____
4. All that God created was _____
5. God can do _____

Answer the following questions:

1. What did God create on day one? _____
2. What did God create on day three? _____
3. What did God create on day five? _____
4. What was God's most important creation? _____
5. What did He breathe into them? _____

Core Sentences:

God created the heavens and the earth.
He is all powerful.
He can do anything.
He created people.
God loves all people.

4. Sin entered the World

Bible Verse*: "When you sin, the pay you get is death. But God gives you the gift of eternal life because of what Christ Jesus our Lord has done." (Romans 6:23)* Read Genesis 3.

God made a beautiful world. He made Adam and Eve without sin. God is holy. So God made them perfect and holy. But they disobeyed God and did what *they* wanted to do. That is called 'sin.' Sin is doing what is wrong. Not obeying God is sin.

God gave Adam and Eve the whole world to enjoy and rule. There was one tree in the garden called the "tree of knowledge of good and evil." God told them not to eat from that tree, *(Genesis 2:15-17.)*

Satan is God's enemy. He wanted Adam and Eve to disobey God. He came like a serpent and **deceived** Eve. The serpent lied to Eve. He told her that she would not die if she ate the fruit. Eve ate the fruit and gave it to Adam also. They both sinned. They now had a **sinful nature**. All the people in the world are born from Adam and Eve. So, every person has a sinful nature.

When Adam and Eve sinned they covered themselves with fig leaves. They were ashamed. They tried to hide from God. God made clothes for them with animal skin and covered them. *(Genesis 3:21.)* That is a picture of Jesus Christ, who died for us. After three days He became alive again. Jesus died to cover the sins of all people who believe in Him and follow Him.

The **wages** for sin is death. *(Romans 6:23.)* Death is **separation** from God. Adam and Eve separated from God in their spirit. Their bodies began to grow old slowly. Later they died physically. They could not live in the Garden of Eden anymore.

God drove them out of the garden. Adam would have to work hard to bring food from the ground. Eve would have much pain in childbirth. God **cursed** the serpent also.

God loves people. He does not want people to be separated from Him. He had a perfect plan to bring people back to Himself. He promised to send a **Savior** or **Deliverer** one day. *(Genesis 3:15.)* Jesus is the Savior who came to this world many years later. Only Jesus can **forgive** our sins and connect us back to God.

Vocabulary:

1. **deceive:** make something wrong seem like the truth
2. **sinful nature:** the part of people that makes them sin
3. **wages:** reward or pay for something you do
4. **curse:** strong words to harm someone, usually because they did something wrong
5. **Savior**: one who saves us from sin and its punishment
6. **forgive:** not remember the wrong things done; set free from wrong done; stop being angry
7. **Deliverer:** someone who will save others from evil

Fill in the blanks:

1. God created Adam and Eve without _____.
2. Adam and Eve _____God.
3. Sin is doing what is _____.
4. Sin _____ us from God.
5. God promised to send a _____.

Answer the following questions:

1. Who deceived Eve? _____
2. What is sin? _____
3. What did Adam and Eve do? _____
4. What was the result? _____
5. Who is the promised Savior? _____

Core Sentences:

Adam and Eve disobeyed God. They were sinners.
We have all descended from Adam and Eve.
So, we also are sinners. Only Jesus Christ can save us.

5.   Noah Chose God's Way

Bible Verse: *"...the Lord was pleased with Noah." (Genesis 6:8)*

Adam and Eve had children. Did these children love and obey God? No. Two of their children were Cain and Abel. Cain got angry and killed his brother, Abel. You can read the story in *Genesis 4:1-16.* Adam and Eve had sinful nature. So their children, Cain and Abel, had sin too. It was **passed down** from **generation** to generation.

Read *Genesis 6: 5-7.* People did not do what God said. They were very sinful. They did many wicked things. God is a holy God. God hates sin. God saw the sins people were doing. God loves people, but sin must be **punished**. God had a plan to **destroy** the world. God said, *"I am going to send a flood on the earth to destroy every living thing. Everything on the earth will die." (Genesis 6:17)*

Only one man, Noah, obeyed God. God was **pleased** with Noah. God had a plan to save Noah and his family. God told Noah to build a huge boat (ark.) Noah and his family would be safe in the ark. God promised to keep them safe. God asked Noah to bring two of every kind of animal and living thing into the boat. There was only one door on the ark. All who came into the ark by that door would be safe.

God sent rain on the earth for forty days and forty nights. There was a huge flood. People were very wicked. They did not follow God. They did not obey God. They did not get into the ark. They were destroyed in the flood. But God saved Noah and his family.

After the flood water went down, Noah, his family and all the living things in the ark came out on to dry ground.   God promised Noah that He would never again destroy the world by flood. He put a **rainbow** in the sky as a **sign** of His promise. *(Genesis 9:13-17)* God always keeps His promises.

The ark is a picture of God's plan to save us from our sins. Just as Noah's ark had only one door, there is only one door or one way to get to heaven and be saved from hell. Jesus said, "I am the door." We can enter heaven only through faith in Him.

Vocabulary:

1. **passed down:** given to children, grand-children, to all generations
2. **generation:** all the people living at one time, for about thirty years
3. **punish:** hurt someone in order to help them; discipline
4. **please:** to make someone happy
5. **rainbow:** a curved line of many colors in the sky after rain
6. **sign:** picture or words that give information

Fill in the blanks:

1. All people are born with a _____ nature.
2. People did not _____ God.
3. God was _____ with Noah.
4. God wanted to _____ all the wicked people.
5. God _____ Noah and his family.
6. We can _____ heaven only through faith in _____ _____.

Answer the following questions:

1. What did God ask Noah to do? Build _____ _____
2. What was God going to send? _____
3. Why were the people destroyed? _____
4. What did God put in the sky? _____
5. What did God promise? _____

Core Sentences:

Noah and his family believed and obeyed God.
All the other people didn't believe and didn't obey God.
They were destroyed, but God saved Noah and his family.

6.   The Tower of Babel

Bible Verse: *"Then God gave his blessing to Noah and his sons. He said to them, "Have children and increase your numbers. Fill the earth." (Genesis 9:1)*

After the flood waters went down, the ground was dry. Noah, his wife, their three sons and their wives came out of the ark. All the living things in the ark also came out. God told them to "fill the earth" *(Genesis 9:1)*

Noah's sons had children and after many years there were a large number of people in the world. Did they obey God? No. *"Then they said, "Come. Let's build a city for ourselves. Let's build a tower that reaches to the sky. We'll* **make a name** *for ourselves. Then we won't be* **scattered over the face** *of the whole earth." (Genesis 11:4)*

God had told them to, "Fill the earth." They did not obey God. They stayed in one place. They decided to stay together and build a city. They decided to build a very big tower and stay together.

God saw what the people were doing. He was not pleased with what they were doing. They were disobeying Him. He stopped them from building the tower. How did He do that? At that time all the people spoke one language. He made all of them speak in different languages. God **confused** their language.

They could not communicate with each other. They did not understand each other. They could not work together to build the tower. They had to stop building the tower. That tower is called "The Tower of **Babel.**" That is where God confused the language of the people. Those who could understand each other stayed together. Then each group went to live in different parts of the country. Over many years they **migrated** to other parts of the world. They formed into many nations.

God can do anything. He is all powerful. What He has planned will happen. He promised to send a deliverer to save the people from their sins. He loves people of all nations. God's plan was to choose one group of people from whom the Deliverer would come. He would be the Deliverer for people of all nations.

Vocabulary:

1. **make a name:** become famous
2. **scatter:** go to many different places, separate and go in different directions
3. **over the face of:** surface; on top of
4. **confuse:** mix up; not able to understand
5. **babel**: confusing noise
6. **migrate:** to move from one area or country to another

Fill in the blank:

1. God told Noah and his family to _____ the earth.
2. The people dis_____ God.
3. They started building a _____.
4. God _____ them from building the tower.
5. He made them speak different _____.

Answer the following questions:

1. What did God tell Noah's descendants? _____
2. What did they do? _____
3. Were they successful? _____
4. What did God do? _____
5. What does this tell us about God? _____

Core Sentences:

God told the people to, "Fill the earth."
The people stayed together and built a tower.
God saw what they were doing and He stopped them.
He confused their language. They had to scatter.
God can do anything. His plans never fail.

7.   Abram had Faith in God

Bible Verse: *"Abram believed the Lord. The Lord accepted Abram because he believed.   So his faith made him right with the Lord."* *(Genesis 15:6)*

Noah's sons were Shem, Ham and Japheth. Abram was one of Shem's **descendants.** Abram lived about 2000 **B.C.** (before Christ.) Abram had **faith** in God. He **believed** what God said. He had trust in God.

God loves people of all nations. He wants all people to know the good news about the Savior who would come. He chose one man, Abram, to be part of His plan. This story happened about 4000 years ago. God called Abram and promised him many **blessings.**

God told Abram to leave his family and country. God would show Abram where he should go. God made some great promises to Abram. God would give great blessings to Abram if he obeyed.

God promised Abram many blessings. (1) He would make Abram's descendants a great nation. At that time Abram was 75 years old and childless. (2) He would make Abram's name great. (3) He would greatly bless Abram and **protect** him by His power. (4) God promised Abram that *"...All nations on earth will be blessed because of you." (Genesis 12:3b)* This was the greatest promise to Abram. It was about the Savior.   The promise meant that the Savior will be a descendant of Abram. He would save all people, by defeating sin, Satan and all evil. All nations and people on earth will be blessed when they believe in the Savior.

In *Genesis 12:7,* God made another promise to Abram. God promised to give the land of Canaan to Abram and his descendants. Canaan is Israel now. God always keeps His promises.

God kept all the promises He made to Abram. God changed Abram's name to 'Abraham,' which means "father of many (nations.)" God rewarded Abraham with many blessings. Abraham believed God. He was **righteous** before God. Abraham pleased

God by his faith. We please God when we have faith in the Lord Jesus and follow Him.

Vocabulary:

1. **descendant:** come from; future generations; come from ancestor
2. **B.C.:** before the birth of Christ
3. **faith:** belief in God from the heart; believing God can do great things
4. **believe:** to think someone or something is true; to trust; have faith
5. **blessing:** something good said to someone, good things promised by God
6. **righteous:** right before God; accepted by God

Fill in the blanks:

1. God promised Abram many _____.
2. Abram had _____ in God. He believed what God said.
3. God told Abram, "...All _____ on _____ will be blessed because of you." *(Genesis 12:3b)*
4. Abram had faith in God. He o_____ God.
5. God b_____ Abram with many blessings.

Answer the following questions:

1. What did God tell Abram to do? _____
2. What did Abram do? _ _____
3. What did God promise Abram? _____
4. What was the greatest promise? _____
5. How did Abram please God? _____

Core Sentences:

Abram had faith in God.
Abram obeyed God.
God blessed Abram.
God promised to make him a great nation.
All nations of the earth would be blessed through Abraham.

8.   Isaac, Abraham's Son

Bible Verse: *""Sometime later God put Abraham to the test. He said to him, "Abraham!" "Here I am," Abraham replied. Then God said, "Take your son, your only son. He is the one you love. Take Isaac. Go to Moriah. Give him to me there as a burnt offering. Sacrifice him on one of the mountains I will tell you about.""* (Genesis 22:1-2)

God had promised to Abraham that he would be the father of many nations. But, Abraham and his wife, Sarah, were childless. Did God forget His promises to Abraham? No. God never forgets His promises. He will always keep His promises. God is all powerful. He can do anything.

When Abraham was 100 years old and Sarah was 90, a child was born to them. They were very happy that God had blessed them with a son, Isaac. God rewarded their faith. God loved them very much.

A few years later, God tested Abraham's faith. God loved him and Isaac. God told Abraham to take his only son Isaac and **sacrifice** him on the mountain. That was very hard for Abraham. But he was **willing** to obey God. He believed God loved them. He believed that God would keep His promise. He believed that God would give him back his son. Abraham had great faith in God.

Early in the morning, Abraham and Isaac went up the mountain. There Abraham built an **altar** and tied Isaac to that altar. He **lifted** his knife to sacrifice Isaac. But God stopped him. God called out from heaven, "Do not lay a hand on the boy," He said, "Do not do anything to him." God told Abraham not to kill his son. God saved Isaac. God was pleased that Abraham had faith in Him and obeyed Him. God was pleased that Abraham loved Him above all.

God showed Abraham a **ram** that was **caught** in the bush nearby. Abraham took the ram and sacrificed it to God. Then Abraham and Isaac went home. They were happy that God loved them and saved Isaac. They were happy that God gave them a ram for the sacrifice.

It was a reminder of the Savior who would come. He would die as a sacrifice for the sins of the world. He would die in our place. We are sinners. We deserve to die. But Jesus died in our place. He is our **substitute**. Now we can live forever if we believe in Jesus. When we repent of our sins, accept Him and follow His ways, we will belong to God's family.

Vocabulary:

1. **sacrifice:** to give up something important for someone else
2. **willing:** decide to do something; say 'yes' to do something
3. **altar:** place to put gifts for God
4. **lifted:** to raise; to bring from a lower to a higher place.
5. **ram:** a male sheep
6. **caught:** captured; cannot move
7. **substitute:** take the place of another person, exchange

Fill in the blanks:

1. Isaac was the _____ of Abraham and Sarah.
2. God _____ Abraham's faith.
3. He told Abraham to _____ Isaac.
4. Abraham _____ God.
5. God did not let Abraham _____ Isaac.
6. Abraham's _____ pleased God.

Answer the following questions:

1. What did God ask Abraham to do with Isaac? _____
2. What did Abraham do? _____
3. Did God allow Isaac to die? _____
4. What substitute for Isaac did God give? _____
5. Who is our substitute? _____

Core Sentences:

Abraham loved God above all.
God tested Abraham's faith in Him.
Abraham obeyed God.

9.   Joseph was sold and taken to Egypt

Bible Verse: *"He (God) saved Joseph from all his troubles. God made Joseph wise. He helped him to become the friend of Pharaoh, the king of Egypt. So, Pharaoh made Joseph ruler over Egypt and his whole palace." (Acts 7:10)*

Isaac had two sons, Esau and Jacob. God **changed** Jacob's name to 'Israel.' Israel became the father of the families of the nation of Israel. Jacob had twelve sons. Joseph was very special to his father, Jacob. Jacob made a coat of many colors for Joseph. His brothers became jealous of Joseph and hated him.

One day when they were out in the fields, far from their home, the brothers caught Joseph and threw him into a **deep pit**. After some time they took him out and sold him to **merchants** who were going to Egypt. Joseph was only seventeen years old at that time.

Joseph had great faith in God. He believed that God would take care of him. In Egypt, God gave Joseph the **ability** to tell the meaning of dreams.

Pharaoh, the king of Egypt had a dream. Joseph told him the meaning of the dream. The dream was about a **famine** that was coming to Egypt. Before the famine there would be seven years of plenty of food. Joseph advised Pharaoh to prepare for the famine. He told Pharaoh to save up a lot of food before the famine came.

Pharaoh was very pleased with Joseph's answer. He made Joseph a very important man in Egypt. Joseph became very powerful. He was next in position to Pharaoh. Pharaoh trusted Joseph. Joseph followed God's ways. God was with Joseph and blessed him.

Joseph **forgave** his brothers of the wicked things they had done to him. When the famine came, he invited his father, his brothers and their families to come and live in Egypt. There was a lot of food in Egypt for all.

God's plan was to take Joseph to Egypt. Joseph had faith in God. God used him to save many people from **starvation.** One day God would send His Son to save people from their sins, from hell and eternal death. God's plan is to save us from eternal death in hell. Joseph forgave his brothers. God will forgive us when we believe in Jesus Christ and follow Him.

Vocabulary:

1. **change:** make something different
2. **deep:** very far down
3. **pit:** large hole in the ground
4. **merchant:** person who buys and sells things
5. **ability:** can do something very well
6. **famine:** no food anywhere for a long time
7. **forgive:** to make someone free from sins; to stop being angry
8. **starvation:** (noun) not have food to eat

Write YES or NO before the sentences:

1. _____ Joseph's brothers loved him.
2. _____ They threw him into a deep pit.
3. _____ Joseph had great faith in God.
4. _____ Pharaoh did not like Joseph.
5. _____ Joseph forgave his brothers.

Answer the following questions:

1. Why did Joseph's brothers sell him? _____
2. Where was Joseph taken? _____ _____
3. What did Joseph do for Pharaoh? _____
4. What did Pharaoh do for Joseph? _____
5. What did Joseph do for his brothers? _____

Core Sentences:

Joseph was sold by his brothers and taken to Egypt.
Joseph had faith in God. God was with him.
God blessed him and made him a ruler.
Joseph forgave his brothers.

10.   God called Moses

The Israelites lived in Egypt for 210 years. They grew to be a large number of people. There came a new Pharaoh in Egypt. He did not like the Israelites living in Egypt. So he made them **slaves.** The Egyptians **treated** the Israelites very badly. But God blessed the Israelites and they increased in number. Pharaoh did not like that. He made a new law that all newborn Israelite baby boys should be thrown into the river Nile.

During this time, a baby boy was born in a Hebrew (Israelite) family. They did not want to throw the baby in the river. The mother made a floating basket. She put the baby in the basket and let him **float** down the river. The daughter of Pharaoh came to the river to bathe. She saw the basket with the baby in it. She wanted the baby to be her child. So, she took the baby to the palace and named him "Moses." Moses was **raised** as a prince in Pharaoh's palace.

God had saved Moses from death. He had a special plan for Moses. The Israelites cried to God for help and God heard their cry. He wanted them to be free. He would **deliver** them from Pharaoh. He would take them back to Canaan. That is what He had promised Abraham. God loves His people. He always keeps His promises. He chose Moses to lead His people out of Egypt and into Canaan, just as He had promised Abraham.

When Moses was 40 years old, he **visited** the place where the Hebrew (Israelite) people were working. He saw that they were being treated badly by the Egyptians. He got very angry and killed the Egyptian who was beating one of the Hebrews. Then he **fled** to the land called Midian.

Moses lived in Midian for 40 years. He became a shepherd. One day he saw a burning **bush,** but it was not getting burned up. As he went near the bush to see why it was not getting burned up, he heard God calling him. God told Moses, *"I am the God of your father, the God of Abraham, Isaac, and Jacob." (Exodus 3:6.)* Then He told Moses that He had seen the suffering of His people. He had heard their cry for help and wanted to **rescue** them. He told Moses to go to Pharaoh and tell him that God wanted him to free the Israelites.

He chose Moses to be their **leader** to deliver them from Egypt. God promised to be with him. God had promised that one day He would send a Deliverer who would save all people from their sins. Do you know who that Deliverer is? That Deliverer is Jesus Christ. He will save anyone who will believe in Him.

Vocabulary:

1. **slaves**: people forced to work for someone else
2. **treat**: to behave toward someone in a certain way
3. **float**: to move or rest on the surface of a liquid without sinking
4. **raised**: the way a child grows up in a family
5. **deliver**: become free
6. **visit**: to go to see someone and spend time with them
7. **fled**: run away to escape bad result
8. **bush**: a plant, smaller than a tree and has many branches
9. **rescue**: to deliver or save from danger
10. **leader**: somebody whom people follow

Answer the following questions:

1. How were the Israelites treated by the Egyptians? _____
2. Who rescued baby Moses from the river?_____
3. Why did Moses kill an Egyptian? _____
4. What did God tell Moses from the burning bush?_____
   _____
5. What did God promise Moses, when he was afraid to go to Pharaoh? _____

Core Sentences:

God called Moses to deliver His people.
God promised to be with him.
Moses believed and obeyed God.
God used Moses to deliver His people.
Jesus Christ is our Deliverer.

11.   The Israelites were Slaves in Egypt
First Nine Plagues

Bible Verse: *"Then the Lord said to him, (to Abraham) "You can be sure of what I am about to tell you. Your children who live after you will be strangers in a country that does not belong to them. They will become slaves . . . But I will punish the nation that makes them slaves... Your children's grandchildren will come back here."*
(Genesis 15: 13, 14, 16a)

The Israelites were slaves in Egypt. The Egyptians **treated** the Israelites very badly. They cried to God for help and God heard their cry. He wanted them to be free. He would deliver them from Pharaoh. He would take them back to Canaan. That is what He had promised Abraham.

He chose Moses to be their leader to lead them out of Egypt. God promised Moses that his brother, Aaron, would help him. Moses and Aaron went to Pharaoh, the king of Egypt. Moses told Pharaoh that God had sent a message for him. Pharaoh must let the Israelites go free. But Pharaoh refused to let them go. He made the Israelites work harder for him.

God began sending many **plagues** on Egypt. This was to make Pharaoh free the Israelites. God told Moses to go to the Nile River and touch the water with his **rod**. The Nile River, which they **worshipped**, turned into blood. All the water in Egypt turned into blood. God also sent other plagues over the whole land of Egypt. There came the plagues of frogs, **gnats**, flies, death of animals, boils, hail, locusts and darkness. All the Egyptians suffered. But God kept the Israelites safe from the plagues. God protects and takes care of people who have faith in Him.

When each plague came on Egypt, Pharaoh called Moses. He asked Moses to pray that God would take away the plague. He promised to let the Israelites go. Moses prayed to God and God stopped the plague. Each time Pharaoh changed his mind and refused to let the people go.

God was very **patient**. When Pharaoh continued to say, "No," God sent the **worst** plague on the Egyptians. God made Pharaoh free His people. God's plans never fail. All things are **possible** with God. He loves us and wants to free us from our sins. He will forgive our sins when we put our faith in His Son, the Lord Jesus Christ. He will protect us from hell and destruction.

Vocabulary:

1. **treat:** to behave toward someone in a certain way
2. **plagues:** something very bad that happens to all the people
3. **rod:** a narrow round stick, made of wood or metal
4. **worship:** to give honor and respect to God or to an idol
5. **gnats:** small insects
6. **patient:** to be kind and wait
7. **worst:** the most bad thing that happened
8. **possible:** able to do something

Fill in the blanks:

1. The Israelites were _____ in Egypt.
2. God called Moses to _____ the Israelites out of Egypt.
3. _____ did not let them go.
4. God sent many_____.
5. Pharaoh _____ to let them go.

Answer the following questions:

1. Where did the Israelites live as slaves? _____
2. What did they ask God? _____
3. Who did God send to deliver them? _____
4. What did God send on Egypt? (one word) _____
5. Did Pharaoh free the Israelites after the nine plagues? _____

Core Sentence:

All things are possible with God.
God can do anything.
He is all powerful.

12.   God Delivered the Israelites – the Passover

Bible Verse: *"The Lord had spoken to Moses. He had said, "I will bring one more plague on Pharaoh and on Egypt." (Exodus 11:1)*

The Israelites were slaves in Egypt for about 100 years. Pharaoh, the ruler of Egypt, refused to free the Israelites. God sent many plagues on Egypt. Finally, God told Moses that He would send the worst plague on Egypt.

God gave the Israelites exact **instructions** on what to do. If they obeyed God they would be saved from the death. Each Israelite family should take a lamb or a goat. It should be a **perfect** lamb, without any **flaws**. The lamb should be killed. The blood was to be allowed to flow out. This was to remind the Israelites that the **punishment** for sin is death.

They had to take some of the blood and put it on the sides and tops of the **doorframe** of their houses. Everyone should stay inside the house. God said that on that night He would pass through the land. If He saw blood on the door of the house then the death angel would not kill the first-born in that house. Every house that had blood on the doorframes would be safe. No one inside the house would die.

That night the death angel passed over all of Egypt. In every home the oldest son died. This was God's **judgment** on them. But in the homes of the Israelites no one died. They were safe, because they had the blood of the lamb on their doorframe. The death angel "passed over" their homes.

That night, Pharaoh's first-born son also died. Pharaoh had great **sorrow.** He knew that the God of the Israelites was very powerful. He can do anything. Pharaoh called Moses and told him to take the people and leave Egypt **immediately.**

Moses led the Israelites out of Egypt. They were very happy. They praised God who had delivered them out of slavery. They were free. God had delivered them as He had promised. Jesus Christ is called the, "Lamb of God who takes away the sins of the world." He is also called the "Passover Lamb." He is the sinless, pure and holy Son of God who died in our place. Now if you have faith that Jesus died in your place and became alive again, God's judgment will pass over you. You will not go to hell and be separated from God. You can go to be with God in heaven and live forever in peace and joy.

Vocabulary:

1. **instruction:** tell someone what to do
2. **perfect:** 100% correct
3. **flaw:** not perfect, something wrong
4. **punishment:** bad thing done to those who do wrong
5. **doorframe:** wood around the door
6. **judgment:** God's punishment for sin
7. **sorrow:** very sad
8. **immediately:** without waiting; without delay; at once

Fill in the blanks:

1. Pharaoh _____ to free the Israelites.
2. All the first-_____ in Egypt would _____.
3. God told the Israelites to kill a _____ lamb or goat.
4. The Israelites put the blood of the lamb on their ____ _____.
5. God did not _____ their first-born. The Angel of Death _____ _____ the house which had blood on the door posts.

Answer the following questions:

1. How many plagues did God send on Egypt? _____
2. What was the last plague? _____
3. Why were the Israelites safe? _____
4. What happened to Pharaoh's first-born son? _____
5. What did Pharaoh do to the Israelites when his son died? _____
_____

Core Sentence:

Jesus is our Passover Lamb.
He died, so we can live.

13. God Gave the Ten Commandments

Bible Verse: *"Here are all of the words God spoke. He said, 'I am the Lord your God. I brought you out of Egypt. That is the land where you were slaves.'" (Exodus 20:1-2)*

The Israelites left Egypt and **crossed** the Red Sea. God made a **path** in the Red Sea so they could cross it. They journeyed for a long time. God gave them food and water every day. In the day time, He was in a pillar of cloud to guide them. At night, He was in a pillar of fire to give them light. He was with them day and night.

They were a large nation. God had chosen Moses to be their leader. God wanted the Israelites to have a close relationship with Him. God loved them and He wanted them to love Him and other people. God is holy, so He wanted the Israelites to be holy. God gave them the Ten **Commandments.**

When the people reached Mt. Sinai, God called Moses to go up the mountain. There Moses met with God. There God gave Moses the Ten Commandments. God wrote them on two **tablets** of stone.

Here are the Ten Commandments

1. "Do not put any other gods in place of me.
2. Do not make **statues** of gods that look like anything in the sky or on the earth or in the waters. Do not bow down to them or worship them.
3. Do not **misuse** the name of the Lord your God.
4. Remember to keep the Sabbath day holy.
5. **Honor** your father and mother.
6. Do not commit murder.
7. Do not commit **adultery**.
8. Do not steal.
9. Do not give **false witness** against your neighbor.
10. Do not **long for** anything that belongs to your neighbor."

The Israelites did not always obey these commandments of God. Why? They had sinful nature as Adam and Eve, who sinned. We have all sinned. We need a Savior. That Savior is Jesus Christ. He will save all who believe in Him. He will forgive their sins.

Vocabulary:

1. **path:** way to go from one place to another
2. **cross it:** to go over to the other side
3. **commandment:** laws; what one is told to do
4. **tablet:** a thick, flat piece of stone to write on
5. **statue:** an image (made like someone or an animal) made with stone, wood or metal
6. **misuse:** use in a wrong way
7. **honor:** respect someone
8. **adultery:** having sex with someone who is not your spouse
9. **false witness:** tell a lie against someone
10. **long for:** want something very much

Fill in the blanks:

1. God gave the Israelites _____ and _____ as they traveled.
2. God guided them in a _____ during the day time.
3. He was in a pillar of fire at night to _____ them _____.
4. God gave them the _____ _____.
5. God said, "Do not put any other _____ in place of me.

Answer the following questions:

1. How did the Israelites cross the Red Sea? _____
2. Who was their leader? _____
3. What is the fifth commandment? _____
4. Did the Israelites <u>always</u> obey God? _____
5. Why did they not obey God always? _____

Core Sentences:

The Israelites didn't always obey God's laws.
We also don't obey Him always. We need a Savior.

14.   The Tabernacle and the Temple

Bible Verse: *"He must make the Most Holy Room, the Tent of Meeting and the altar pure. And he must pay for the sin of the priests and all of the people in the whole community." (Leviticus 16:33)*

Moses went up on Mount Sinai to receive the Ten Commandments from God.   God wanted Moses to build a **tabernacle**. A tabernacle was a tent that could be moved. It was a place of worship and sacrifice to God. It is also called a "Holy Tent." It had to be made **exactly** the way God told Moses.

The tabernacle had a large fence around it. It had only one door to enter. It had two main rooms in it. The first room was called "the Holy Room." The rooms were divided by a thick curtain. The **curtain** was a **reminder** that sin separates us from God.

The second room was called the "Most Holy Room." In the second room was the **Ark**. The Ark (not Noah's ark) was a wooden box. It was covered with gold all over the inside and outside. The lid of the box had two angels on it. They were made of pure gold. The top of the box was called the '**mercy** seat.'

Once a year, the High Priest had to make himself clean. He must go into the Most Holy Room. He must bring the blood of a lamb. He must **sprinkle** the blood of the lamb on the lid of the ark. Then God forgave his sins and the sins of the people. A lamb had died for their sins. Jesus Christ is called the "Lamb of God." He died in our place. When He died on the cross, the thick curtain in the temple tore, from top to bottom. Jesus made a way for us to be connected with God again.

After many years, the Israelites reached the land God had promised them. They had many judges and **prophets** to rule them. Then they wanted a king like other countries. They kept asking. So God gave them kings.

The name of their second king was David. Solomon, the son of King David, built a **magnificent** temple for God. He built it exactly as God told him to. God told King Solomon to have a very large area in the **temple** called the "Court of the Nations." There, people from all nations could come and learn about the one true God. God wants people everywhere to know Him.

Vocabulary:

1. **tabernacle:** a place used to worship and sacrifice to God
2. **exactly:** 100%; without any change
3. **curtain:** a piece of cloth hung on window or door
4. **Ark:** a wooden box, covered in gold
5. **mercy:** kindness or forgiveness given to a wrong doer
6. **sprinkle:** put a little of the liquid over something or someone
7. **prophet:** someone who speaks for God
8. **magnificent:** very, very beautiful and grand
9. **temple:** a place used for worship of God

Fill in the blanks:

1. _____ told Moses to build a tabernacle.
2. The tabernacle had only _____ door.
3. The second room was called the Most _____ _____.
4. The priest had to _____ the blood on the ark.
5. Then God _____ the sins of the people.

Answer the following questions:

1. What did God ask Moses to make? _____
2. What is a tabernacle?_____
3. What divided the two main rooms?_____
4. What was the second room called? _____
5. Who built the first temple? _____

Core Sentences:

God made a way for the Israelites to be connected to Him.
Jesus Christ is the only way we can be connected to God.

15.   The Israelites in the Promised Land

Bible Verse: *"Then the Lord said to him, (to Abraham) "You can be sure of what I am about to tell you. Your children who live after you will be strangers in a country that does not belong to them. They will become slaves. They will be treated badly for 400 years. But I will punish the nation that makes them slaves...Your children's grandchildren will come back here." (Genesis 15: 13, 14, 16a)*

God delivered the Israelites out of Egypt. Moses was their leader. God led them to Mt. Sinai. There He gave them the Ten Commandments. Then He led them to the southern **tip** of the land of Canaan. God had promised Abraham that He would bring his **descendants** back to Canaan.

Moses chose twelve men from the twelve **tribes** of Israel. They had to go and **spy** out the land. When the men returned, they brought back huge **bunches** of fruit from Canaan. They reported to Moses and the people that Canaan was a very rich land. But, the people who lived there were huge and tall. They were also very powerful. Ten of the spies were afraid and said the Israelites could never defeat them.

Two of the men were Joshua and Caleb. They believed that God would help them defeat the Canaanites. They had faith in God's promises. They believed that God would give them the land, just as He had promised Abraham.

The people did not listen to Joshua and Caleb. They believed the bad report of the other ten men. They began to **complain** against Moses and against God. They did not want to go to Canaan and fight the giants. They wanted to go back to Egypt. Their complaining made God very sad and angry. He said that those who complained and did not believe would not enter the Promised Land.

They had to **wander** in the **desert** for forty years, till they all died. That was their punishment. Then God took their children into the Promised Land.

After Moses died, Joshua became their leader. Joshua trusted in God. God helped Joshua and the Israelites to defeat the enemies in Canaan. Then Canaan became the land of the Israelites. God kept His promise to Abraham. He has promised to take to heaven all who believe and follow Him. God always keeps His promises.

Vocabulary:

1. **tip:** edge; at one end
2. **descendants:** future generations; come from ancestor
3. **tribe:** a group of people who have common culture
4. **spy:** to get information secretly
5. **bunch:** many things put together
6. **complain:** to express discontent or unhappiness about a situation
7. **desert:** dry and sandy place, where there is no water
8. **wander:** to travel without going any place

Fill in the blanks:

1. Twelve _____ were sent to Canaan.
2. Ten brought back bad _____.
3. Two of them _____ God's promise.
4. All the people _____ against God and _____.
5. They had to _____ in the desert for _____ years.

Answer the following questions:

1. How many spies did Moses send into Canaan?_____
2. How many believed in God's promises?_____
3. Most of them didn't believe God. What did they do? _____
4. What did God do because they did not believe Him? _____
   _____
5. What did God do for their children? _____

Core Sentences:

God gave Canaan to the Israelites as He had promised Abraham.
God has promised Heaven to all who believe in Jesus Christ.

16.   The Prophecies

Bible Verse: *"He himself will set Israel free from all of their sins."*
(Psalm 130:8)

God helped the Israelites to defeat their enemies. Canaan became their land. They had judges to rule them. After many years, they asked God for a king. One of their kings was King Solomon. He built the first temple for God. He built it just as God told him to. The king followed God's ways. After sometime, he began to disobey God. He turned away from God. He chose his own way.

After he died, the Israel nation became **divided**. They became two **separate** kingdoms. The northern **kingdom** was called Israel. The southern kingdom was called Judah. Many of their kings did not follow God's ways. But some did. They continued to believe in God and the coming Messiah.

Most of the kings were **wicked** and evil. So, most of the people followed their evil ways. The people turned away from the one true God. They began to worship **idols**. They did not obey the first and second commandment God had given them. God was very displeased with the people and what they were doing.

God still loved them. He wanted them to turn back to Him. So, He sent many **prophets** to them. They warned the people of the coming **judgment** of God, if they didn't repent. They also **prophesied** the good news about the Deliverer, who was coming. The last prophet was Malachi. After him, God did not send any prophets for 400 years. God did not send any message to them. After those years of silence, God sent His own Son, the Deliverer.

There are more than 300 prophecies about the Deliverer in the Old Testament. All of them were written about 400 – 1000 years before He was born. Each one of the prophecies came true when God sent the Deliverer into this world.

More than 2000 years ago, God sent the Lord Jesus Christ. He came to deliver us from our sins, from Satan and from hell. He wants to forgive the sins of all those who will believe in Him, turn away from their sins and follow Him. Be sure to study Book 2. You will learn about Jesus Christ and His life. It's all part of God's **wonderful** plan for you.

Vocabulary:

1. **divide**: to make into two or more parts
2. **separate:** not together; different
3. **kingdom:** a state or people ruled by a king or queen
4. **wicked:** very bad; evil
5. **idols:** a statue or image that is worshiped as a god
6. **prophet:** someone who tells others what God has said
7. **judgment:** result of doing good or bad
8. **prophecy:** saying something that will happen in the future
9. **wonderful:** very, very good

Write YES or NO before the sentences:

1. _____ King Solomon followed God **all** his life.
2. _____ Some kings continued to believe in God.
3. _____ The people began to worship idols.
4. _____ God was not happy with their worship of idols.
5. _____ God sent many prophets to warn them.

Answer the following questions:

1. Who did the people turn away from?_____
2. What did they do? _____
3. Why did God send the prophets? _____
4. What good news did they prophecy? _____
5. How many prophecies are there about the Deliverer?_____

Core Sentences:

God loves His people. He promised to send a Savior.
God's Word is true. He will do what He says.

17.   How to belong to God's Family

Bible Verse: *Jesus replied, "What I'm about to tell you is true. No one can see God's kingdom without being born again." (John 3:3)*

Nicodemus came to Jesus one night. He wanted to know the truth from Jesus. Jesus told Nicodemus that *"no one can see God's kingdom without being born again." (John 3:3.)* Nicodemus was surprised at what Jesus said. *"How can I be born when I am old?" Nicodemus asked. "I can't go back inside my mother! I can't be born a second time!" (John 3:4.)*

Jesus explained that to go to heaven, or see **God's kingdom**, he must be born again. The first time we have physical birth. We are born into this world. We are human beings. We are born into a human family. When Adam and Eve sinned they were separated from God. So, all people have sin and are separated from God. All human beings have come from Adam and Eve. They were the first parents. To belong to God's family, we must have **spiritual** birth. We can be **connected** back to God by repenting of our sins and believing that Jesus died and **rose again** to pay for our sins.

When we have physical birth, we are born physically into this world. We must have a spiritual birth to be born into God's family. Sin has **separated** us from God. Jesus Christ, God's Son came into this world to connect us back to God. Jesus told Nicodemus, *"God loved the world so much that he gave his one and only Son. Anyone who believes in him will not die but will have eternal life." (John 3:16)*

To be born again, you must believe that Jesus is the Son of God. You must believe that He came to save you from your sins. If you admit that you are a sinner, turn away from your sins (repent) and accept Jesus to be your Savior, you will be born again spiritually, into God's family. You will be connected back to God in your spirit. His Holy Spirit will come inside you and make you a new person. He will help you keep God's commandments.

You can pray and ask God right now to save you. You must repent (turn away from your sins) and believe that Jesus died and rose again to pay the punishment for your sins. Then He will take away your sins.   You will become a child of God. You will have great peace and joy in your life. Decide now to put your faith in Jesus and do His teachings. When you die and leave this world, you will go to live with God in heaven forever. Heaven is a wonderful place. That is good news!

The sad news is that if you don't choose to repent and believe in Jesus Christ, you will be separated from God forever in hell. Hell is a place where Satan and all the demons will be. It is a place of great suffering and loneliness.

The choice is yours! God invites you to come to Him and He's waiting for you. He loves you very, very much!

Vocabulary:

1. **God's kingdom:** place or area where God is ruler
2. **spiritual:**   that which is related to the soul or spirit
3. **connected:** related to; joined to
4. **separated:** not joined; not in the same place
5. **Savior:** someone who rescues or saves us from danger
6. **rose again:** become alive again after being dead

Fill in the blanks:

1. Nicodemus came to talk to Jesus at _____.
2. Jesus told him, "You must be _____ _____."
3. We can belong to God's family by having spiritual b_____.
4. We are born again when we b_____ on the Lord Jesus Christ.
5. He will _____ our sins if we ask Him to.

"Some people did accept him. They believed in his name. He gave them the right (the power, authority) to become children of God."
John 1:12

To be continued...

Be sure to read the rest of the stories in <u>Book 2 - New Testament.</u> You will learn about the Savior who was promised in the Old Testament. God kept His promise. Jesus Christ, the promised Savior, came into this world!

Here is a website where you can read about God's plan in your own language:

http://www.gotquestions.org/way-of-salvation.html

You can read the Bible in your language here:

http://www.biblegateway.com/versions/

If you would like to talk to someone, you can contact Lakeview Baptist Church. The address is:

Lakeview Baptist Church
1600 East Glenn Avenue
Auburn, AL 36830

Phone #: 334-887-7094

http://www.lakeviewbaptist.org

Appendices

A. Some Bible verses for each lesson
B. Answers to questions in each lesson
C. Teacher's Guide
D. Dictionary of Vocabulary Words

Appendix A

Bible passages to read for each lesson

Lesson   1 - God speaks to us: Psalm 119:105; Isaiah 40:8;
          Galatians 1:11; 2 Peter 1:20-21.
Lesson   2 - God and Creation of Angels: Colossians 1:16;
          Revelation 4:11
Lesson   3 - God is the Creator: Genesis 1 and 2
Lesson   4 - Sin entered the World: Genesis 3
Lesson   5 - Noah chose God's Ways: Genesis 6, 7 and 8
Lesson   6 - The Tower of Babel: Genesis 11:1-8
Lesson   7 - Abram had faith in God: Genesis 12:1-7
Lesson   8 - Isaac, Abraham's Son: Genesis 22: 1-19
Lesson   9 - Joseph was sold and taken to Egypt: Genesis 37-45
Lesson 10 - God called Moses: Exodus 1, 2, 3: 1-12
Lesson 11 - The Israelites were slaves in Egypt: Exodus 7:1-10:29
Lesson 12 - God delivered the Israelites; Exodus 11:1-12:42
Lesson 13 - God gave the Ten Commandments: Exodus 20:1-21
Lesson 14 - The Tabernacle and the Temple: Leviticus 16
Lesson 15 - The Israelites entered the Promised Land: Joshua 3
Lesson 16 - The Prophecies: 2 Peter 1:19-21
Lesson 17 - How to belong to God's Family: John 3; John 1:12

Some characteristics of God:

God is holy: Isaiah 6:1, 2; Psalms 99:5; Psalms 86:8-10;
          Psalms 99:1-3; Isaiah 40:25; 57:15.
God hates sin: Isaiah 59:1, 2, Psalms 66:18, Revelation 21:27,
          Romans 6:23.
God is good: Psalms 145:8-9; Nahum 1:7; Luke. 6:36; James 1:17;
          1 John 1:5; 1 John 4:8.
God is all knowing: 2 Chronicles 16:9a; Psalms 33:13;
          Psalms 147:5; Psalms 139; Isaiah 55:8-9;
          Proverbs 15:3; Romans 11:33.
God is all powerful: Job 33:4; Psalms. 89:8; Isaiah 51:15;
          Hosea 12:5; Amos 5:14 Revelation 16:7;
          Revelation 19:6.
God keeps His promises: Gen. 9:11; Numbers 23:19; Joshua 23:14;
          1 King 8:56; Romans 4:21; Titus 1:2; Hebrews 6:18.

Appendix B

Answers to questions in each lesson

Lesson 1 – God Speaks to us.

1. The Bible is the Word of God.
2. It is a sacred book. It has God's message to us.
3. God communicates with us when we read it.
4. We can read in the Bible that God loves us.
5. He came to be our Savior; to save us from our sins.

Lesson 2 – God and Creation of Angels

1. God. He is all powerful.
2. God hates sin.
3. Satan rebelled against God. He wanted to be God.
4. He was expelled from heaven.
5. Satan wants us to disobey God.

Lesson 3 – God is the Creator

1. On day one God created day and night.
2. On day three God created land, sea and all the plants.
3. On day five God created the sea creatures and birds.
4. God's most important creation was man and woman.
5. God breathed life into them.

Lesson 4 – Sin entered the World

1. Satan came as a serpent and deceived Eve.
2. Sin is disobeying God. All wrongdoing is sin.
3. Adam and Eve sinned. They disobeyed God.
4. They got separated from God in their spirit. Their relationship with God was broken.
5. Jesus Christ is the promised Savior.

Lesson 5 – Noah chose God's Ways

1. Build an ark.
2. God was going to send a flood.
3. They were sinful. They didn't obey God.
4. God put a rainbow in the sky.
5. He promised never to destroy the earth by flood again.

Lesson 6 – the Tower of Babel

1. He told them to 'fill the earth.'
2. They stayed in one place.
3. No.
4. God confused their language.
5. He is all-powerful. He can do anything.

Lesson 7 – Abram had Faith in God

1. God told Abram to leave his family and country.
2. He obeyed God.
3. God promised him many blessings if he obeyed.
4. God promised Abram that *"...All nations on earth will be blessed because of you." (Genesis 12:3b)*
5. Abram pleased God by his faith in Him.

Lesson 8 – Isaac, Abraham's Son

1. God told Abraham to sacrifice his son on the mountain.
2. He obeyed God.
3. No.
4. God showed him a ram that was caught in the bushes.
5. Jesus Christ, God's only Son.

Lesson 9 – Joseph was sold and taken to Egypt

1. They were jealous of him and hated him.
2. He was taken to Egypt.
3. Joseph told Pharaoh the meaning of his dreams.
4. Pharaoh made Joseph a very important man in Egypt.
5. Joseph forgave his brothers.

Lesson 10 – God called Moses

1. They were treated very badly.
2. Pharaoh's daughter rescued baby Moses.
3. Moses killed an Egyptian who was beating an Israelite slave.
4. God told Moses to go and tell Pharaoh to let His people go free.
5. God promised to be with him.

Lesson 11 – the Israelites were slaves in Egypt

1. The Israelites lived as slaves in Egypt.
2. They asked God to help them.
3. Moses.
4. Plagues.
5. No.

Lesson 12 – God delivered the Israelites – the Passover

1. Ten.
2. Death of the first-born.
3. They obeyed God and put the blood of the lamb on their door frames.
4. He died.
5. He told them to leave Egypt immediately.

Lesson 13 – God gave the Ten Commandments

1. God made the water stand up on two sides and made a path in the sea.
2. Moses.
3. Honor your father and your mother.
4. No.
5. They had a sinful nature, like all of us.

Lesson 14 – The Tabernacle and the Temple

1. God told Moses to make a tabernacle or a holy tent.
2. It was a place to worship and sacrifice to God when the Israelites traveled.   God would meet with them there.
3. A thick curtain divided the two rooms.
4. The Most Holy room.
5. King Solomon.

Lesson 15 – The Israelites enter the Promised Land

1. Twelve.
2. Only two believed; Joshua and Caleb.
3. They were afraid and complained.
4. God made them wander in the desert for 40 years till they all died there.
5. God took their children into the Promised Land.

Lesson 16 – The Prophecies

1. They turned away from God.
2. They began to worship idols. They disobeyed the first and second commandments.
3. He wanted them to turn back to Him.
4. They prophesied about the coming Deliverer.
5. More than 300.

Appendix C

Teacher's Guide

This book and Book 2, which has the New Testament stories of Jesus, were written with the main purpose of communicating to the readers how God's plan of salvation through faith in Jesus Christ is revealed right from Genesis. His name is not mentioned in the Old Testament per se, but each story echoes His name and points to the coming Deliverer. The primary goal of these lessons is to teach God's Word. Teaching English is the secondary goal.

Before you begin teaching the lessons in this book, be sure your students know who God is. The attributes that need to be taught here are: *God is love; God is good; God is holy; God hates sin; sin must be punished; God is almighty; God is all-knowing and God keeps His promises*. After each lesson you could ask the students to tell you which attributes of God are brought out in that lesson.

Many books have been written to aid teachers of ESL or ELL students. Following are just a few suggestions to aid you in incorporating some of these methods in teaching the Bible.

1. Preparation is the key to effective teaching and effective student learning. Pray for the Holy Spirit to guide you.

2. Read all of the relevant scriptures for each lesson. Some of these passages are given in Appendix A. Read the story from the book to familiarize yourself with what you'll be reading together with the students.

3. Begin these lessons with introducing the Bible. Briefly explain the structure of the Bible. You may have students who may have never seen a Bible! Explain that the Bible is one book, with many 'books' in it. Turn to the contents and explain the Old and New Testaments. Briefly explain the different sections of the Bible.

4. Tell them that you will begin in Genesis, but you won't always read every verse related to the story. They should

read the scripture for each lesson at home. You will be reading some parts in class. Explain chapter and verse. You may tell them that each verse has its own 'address' or location. Show the students how to find the books of the Bible by looking at the content page.

You may do a 'sword drill.' Choose several scripture verses and write the references on the board. Then ask the students to locate them in their Bibles.

5. Tell the story in your own words, using simple sentences. Have your Bible open. Encourage students to put their pens down and only listen. As you tell the story, on one side of the board, write the words they may not be familiar with. You will be creating a list of vocabulary words to be used later for pronunciation drills.

6. Draw simple pictures as you tell the story. Use other visual aids. It is said, "A picture is worth a thousand words."

7. Read aloud the scripture for each lesson, or parts of it, if too long. Read the lessons together. For the students to learn correct pronunciation, the teacher can read the sentences, one at a time, with the students repeating the same.

8. Do pronunciation drills using the vocabulary list you created earlier and also the ones after each lesson. Go over the meaning of each word. Always explain the words in context. This will give you an opportunity to reinforce the key points in the lesson again. Higher level students can use the words in making their own sentences.

9. If time permits, let the students answer the questions in class. If not, assign as homework. Again, this will be another opportunity to reinforce the lesson.

10. You may write, on the board, six to eight short sentences of the core meaning of the lesson. There are a few core

sentences at the end of each lesson. Use them as 'Jazz Chants' to reinforce the lesson. Keeping a steady rhythm, have the students repeat after you, sentence by sentence. These sentences can also be used to review the lesson.

11.   For basic level students, write questions with short answers on the board. Use them as repetition drills in several ways. You read the questions and they answer. Divide into two groups and each group repeats the question or answer after you.

12.   End each lesson with a short prayer. Give a one or two sentence preview of next lesson and invite students to return to class for the next story.

Appendix D

Dictionary of Vocabulary Words

Note: The meaning of each word below is connected to the lessons in this book. The number of the lesson where each word occurs first is given in brackets.

1. **ability:** can do something very well. (9)
2. **absolutely:** completely, 100%. (3)
3. **adultery:** having sex with someone you are not married to. (13)
4. **almighty:** all powerful, more powerful than anyone. (2)
5. **altar:** place to put gifts for God. (8)
6. **ark**: a wooden box, covered in gold (5)

7. **B.C.:** before the birth of Christ. (7)
8. **babel**: confusing noise. (6)
9. **begin:** to start. (2)
10. **believe:** to think someone or something is true; to trust; have faith. (3)
11. **biography:** written information about someone from birth to death. (1)
12. **bless:** say something good to someone. (7)
13. **blessing:** something good said to someone, good things promised by God. (6)
14. **bunch:** many things put together. (15)
15. **bush:** a plant, smaller than a tree and has many branches. (8)

16. **caught:** captured; cannot move (8)
17. **change:** make something different. (7)
18. **childless:** not have any children born to them. (7)
19. **choose:** decide. (6)
20. **commandment:** laws; what one is told to do. (13)
21. **communicate:** give information to each other, to connect (1)
22. **complain:** to express discontent or unhappiness about a situation. (15)
23. **confuse:** mix up; not able to understand. (6)

24. **create:** make something from nothing. (1)
25. **cross it:** to go over to the other side. (13)
26. **curse:** strong words to harm someone, usually because they did something wrong. (4)
27. **curtain:** a piece of cloth hung on window or door. (14)

28. **deceive:** make something wrong seem like the truth. (4)
29. **decide:** to think and plan. (6)
30. **deep:** very far down. (9)
31. **deliver:** make someone free; save. (10)
32. **deliverer:** someone who will save others from evil. (16)
33. **descendant:** future generations; come from ancestor. (7)
34. **desert:** dry and sandy place, where there is no water. (15)
35. **desire:** to want something very much. (1)
36. **destroy:** to end something; completely gone. (5)
37. **different:** not the same. (1)
38. **divide:** to make into two or more parts. (1)
39. **doorframe:** wood around the door. (12)
40. **drove:** make someone leave a place. (4)

41. **enemy:** somebody who hates another person and wants to harm him or her. (2)
42. **exactly:** 100%; without any change. (2)
43. **explain:** to describe; give information. (17)

44. **faith:** belief in God from the heart; believing God can do great things. (5)
45. **false witness:** tell a lie against someone. (13)
46. **famine:** no food anywhere for a long time. (9)
47. **flaw:** not perfect, something wrong. (12)
48. **fled:** run away to escape bad result. (10)
49. **float:** to move or rest on the surface of a liquid without sinking. (10)
50. **flood:** a lot of water everywhere. (5)
51. **forget:** not remember. (8)

52. **forgive:** not remember the wrong things done; set free from wrong done; stop being angry. (4)
53. **formed:** made. (3)

54. **Genesis:** beginning. (3)
55. **giants:** very tall and big people. (15)
56. **gnats:** small insects. (11)

57. **happen:** something that occurred. (3)
58. **heavens:** space above the earth. (3)
59. **hell**: eternal punishment for Satan and his followers. (1)
60. **holy**: without any sin; completely without any wrongdoing. (1)
61. **honor:** respect someone. (2)

62. **idol:** a statue or image that is worshiped as a god. (11)
63. **immediately:** without waiting; without delay; at once. (12)
64. **immortal:** does not die. **(2)**
65. **important:** of great value; special. (3)
66. **instruction:** tell someone what to do. (12)

67. **journey:** travel. (13)
68. **judgment:** God's punishment for sin, result of doing good or bad. (12)

69. **kingdom:** a state or people ruled by a king or queen. (16)

70. **leader:** somebody whom people follow. (10)
71. **leave:** to go. (7)
72. **lifted:** to raise; to bring from a lower to a higher place. (8)
73. **long for:** want something very much. (13)

74. **magnificent:** very, very beautiful and grand. (14)
75. **make a name:** become famous. (6)
76. **merchant:** person who buys and sells things. (9)
77. **mercy:** kindness or forgiveness given to a wrong doer. (14)

78. **message:** something one person tells or writes to another. (1)
79. **migrate:** to move from one area or country to another. (6)
   misuse: use in a wrong way. (13)
80. **mountain:** a high, rocky place. (8)

81. **over the face of:** surface; on top of. (6)

82. **passed down:** given to children, grand-children, to all generations. (5)
83. **path:** way to go from one place to another. (13)
84. **patient:** to be kind and wait. (11)
85. **perfect:** without evil; 100% correct; does not make mistakes. (4)
86. **personality:** quality or character
87. **physical body:** body of flesh and blood, like that of human beings. (2)
88. **pit:** large hole in the ground. (9)
89. **plagues:** something very bad that happens to all the people. (11)
90. **please:** to make someone happy. (5)
91. **possible:** able to make something happen. (28)
92. **praise:** worship God; say how wonderful He is. (2)
93. **prepare:** make ready. (2)
94. **promise:** agree or not agree to do something. (4)
95. **prophecy:** saying something that will happen in the future. (16)
96. **prophet:** someone who tells others what God has said. (16)
97. **protect:** keep safe; stop enemies from harming you. (7)
98. **proud:** think too highly of oneself. (2)
99. **punish:** hurt someone in order to help them; discipline. (2)
100. **punishment:** bad thing done for those who do wrong. (2)

101. **rainbow:** arc of many colors in the sky after a rain. (5)
102. **raised:** the way a child grows up in a family. (10)
103. **ram:** a male sheep. (7)

104. **reach:** to try and touch. (3)
105. **rebel:** go against a higher authority. (2)
106. **relationship:** to have a connection with; to be close to someone. (1)
107. **remember:** to bring back in your mind. (13)
108. **reminder:** something to make them remember. (14)
109. **repent:** to turn away from sin; to change sinful action. (2)
110. **report:** tell someone what you saw or heard. (15)
111. **reached out:** to stretch
112. **rescue**: to deliver or save from danger. (10)
113. **rest:** remaining; what is left. (1)
114. **reward:** something good that is given for what someone had done. (4)
115. **righteous:** right before God; accepted by God. (7)
116. **rod:** a narrow round stick, made of wood or metal. (11)
117. **rule:** be in control of; in charge of; take care of. (3)

118. **sacred**: holy, belonging to God. (1)
119. **sacrifice:** to give up something important for someone else. (8)
120. **savior:** one who saves; Jesus is the Savior who saves us from our sins and its punishment. (4)
121. **scatter:** go to many different places, separate and go in different directions. (6)
122. **Scripture**: sacred written words; The Holy Bible is the scriptures for Christians. It is God's words for all people. (1)
123. **separate:** not together; in two different places. (4)
124. **serpent:** snake. (4)
125. **sign:** picture or words that give information. (5)
126. **sin:** all wrong doing; not obeying God's words. (1)
127. **sinful nature:** the part of people that makes them sin. (4)
128. **slaves:** people forced to work for someone else. (10)
129. **sorrow:** very sad. (12)
130. **special:** very important; of great value. (3)
131. **spirit:** not natural, like man; spiritual; not human. (2)

132. **sprinkle:** put a little of the liquid over something or someone. (14)
133. **spy:** to get information secretly. (15)
134. **starvation:** (noun) not have any food;
135. **statue:** an image (made like someone or an animal) made with stone, wood or metal. (13)
136. **stay together:** be in one place. (6)
137. **substitute:** take the place of another person, exchange. (8)
138. **suffer:** to have hardship; to feel much pain. (11)

139. **tabernacle:** a tent used by the Israelites, to worship God. (14)
140. **tablet:** a thick, flat piece of stone to write on. (13)
141. **temple:** a place used for worship of God. (14)
142. **tent:** a cover that can be moved (14)
143. **Testament:** a covenant (firm agreement) between God and man. (1)
144. **test:** to find out if what another person thinks is true. (8)
145. **thick:** not thin (14)
146. **tip:** edge; at one end. (15)
147. **tower:** a tall building. (6)
148. **treat:** to behave toward someone in a certain way. (10)
149. **tribe:** a group of people who have common culture. (15)

150. **visit:** to go to see and spend time with somebody. (10)

151. **wages:** reward or pay for something you do. (4)
152. **wander:** to travel without going any place. (15)
153. **wicked:** very bad; evil. (5)
154. **willing:** decide to do something; say 'yes' to do something. (8)
155. **wonderful:** very, very good. (16)
156. **worship:** to give honor, praise and respect to God or to an idol. (2)
157. **worst:** the most bad thing that happened. (11)

~ ~ ~ ~ ~ ~ ~ ~ ~ ~

Made in the USA
Columbia, SC
20 September 2019